DAOS

SOUND
SENSE

SOUND SENSE

Brenda Schaefer

M

First published 1978
Reprinted 1979, 1981, 1982

Published by
MACMILLAN EDUCATION LIMITED
Houndmills, Basingstoke, Hampshire RG21 2XS
and London
Associated companies in
Delhi Dublin Hong Kong
Johannesburg Lagos Melbourne
New York Singapore and Tokyo

ISBN 0 333 25168 7

Printed in Hong Kong

Contents

Preface

A common problem facing many students at junior secondary level is the confusion over the many irregularities in our language. *Sound Sense* has been designed as an aid to overcome these difficulties.

The 35 units of work cover basic sounds through to word study skills. Each unit contains a variety of activities geared specifically to the adolescent who soon loses interest in primary-oriented material.

Many of the activities require the use of a dictionary. This is a deliberate attempt to encourage the student to discover the dictionary as a valuable aid. A spelling component has also been included in many of the units. Words have been grouped in word families to enable students to tackle the problem of spelling in a more logical manner.

1

C Soft and Hard

C is a copycat. It has no personality of its own. Sometimes it copies K. Sometimes it copies S.

Remember

C followed by A/O/U copies K.   can   come   cup

C followed by E/I/Y copies S.   cent   city   fancy

1. DICTIONARY HUNT
    Use your dictionary to find ten more words for each column.

C (A/O/U)	C (E/I/Y)
call	face
coat	cinema
cutlery	cycle

2. SMALL LETTER SENTENCES

    Finish these sentences. The first one is shown as an example.

    (a) Crazy Carol called Craig casually.
    (b) Fancy Nancy ....
    (c) Certain cyclists ....
    (d) The cry came ....
    (e) A creature crept ....
    (f) Carefully Colin ....
    (g) As Christine crocheted ....
    (h) Captain Cook ....
    (i) The city scene ....
    (j) The centennial celebration ....
    (k) My cousin Chris ....

3. WHICH IS WHICH?

    Copy these words into your workbook. Use a red pen to mark the soft C. Use green to mark the hard C.

exercise	centre	cyclone	certain
bicycle	place	circle	cousin
circus	creature	century	crazy
face	economy	arc	crept

4. DETECTIVE WORK

    How many words with a soft C can you find? How many words have a hard C?

    As the clock struck twelve o'clock, the celebrations commenced. A new century had begun. Cynthia and Colin wondered cautiously what the next hundred years would contain. Would there be peace? Would there be crises? Would there be invasions of creatures from outer space? They clung together because an eerie feeling had crept over the crowd.

5. SPELLING
   Arrange these words in alphabetical order, and learn how to spell them. (See unit 30. Remember, 'ce' comes before 'ci', 'cre' comes before 'cro'.)

cinema	bicycle	century
creature	exercise	celebration
crochet	cyclone	carefully
scene	caution	centennial

2

G Soft and Hard

G is a goer. Not content with his own job, he does someone else's work as well.

Remember

G followed by E/I/Y says J.   germ gin   gypsy
G followed by any other letter says G   go   gum gang

1.   DICTIONARY HUNT
     Use your dictionary to find ten more words for each column.

G as G	G as J
game	gentle
good	general
God	age

2. DETECTIVE WORK
Find two words in the paragraph which are exceptions to the rule.

It was a glorious summer day. The young girl wandered amongst the rock pools gathering shells. Suddenly she glimpsed the most gorgeous shell she had ever seen. It was in a deep green pool about a metre away. As she bent over to get a better look, a gold and red striped fish darted from underneath it. As the shell was obviously its home, she was glad to leave it undisturbed.

3. I SPY G WORDS
Play this game in the usual way, but use only words with either a hard or soft G sound.

- I spy with my little eye something that starts with a hard/soft G.
- 1 spy with my little eye something that has a hard /soft G inside the word.

4. SNAP
Make cards using the words which you found in your dictionary hunt. Play snap as usual, matching the hard or soft G sounds.

5. SPELLING
Write these words in alphabetical order, and make sure that you can spell them.

gentle	germ	gathered
general	glimpsed	sergeant
manage	digest	magic
gypsy	regent	margin

5

3

Silent Letters

Letters are like people. Some are noisy and some are quiet. Some letters are so quiet that they make no noise at all.

write

Common silent letters
W   write, wriggle
K   know, knee
G   gnaw, gnome
B   comb, lamb

1. DICTIONARY HUNT
    Use your dictionary to find more words for each column.

W	K	G	B
write	know	gnaw	comb
wrist	knock	gnash	thumb

2. SECRET CODE
   Can you decode this secret message?
   MEETB MEB TONIGHTB ATB SIXB BESIDEB
   THEB TOMB. IB NEEDB YOURB HELPB

   (a) Which word is not in code?
   (b) Make up a code message using a different silent letter.

3. DETECTIVE WORK
   How many silent letters can you find? Beware! There are some less common silent letters hidden in this paragraph.

   John the plumber had a difficult career. He had to know many things and to answer the many questions he received from folk. He had to be able to climb difficult buildings; to wriggle into small places; to wrestle with awkward pipes and to knock difficult joins into place. Many an hour John wondered why he had not chosen another career.

4. SNAP
   Make cards using the words you found in the dictionary hunt. Play snap as usual, matching the same silent letters.

5. SPELLING
   Arrange these words alphabetically, and make sure you can spell them.

   | lamb | comb | wriggle | knee |
   | gnaw | knew | wright | knight |

7

4
QU

Some guys can always be recognized because they hang around with the same mates.

Remember
Q always needs U.
U has lots of other friends.
Q + U makes a KW sound.

1. MIX-UP
    Unscramble the letters to make a word.

    (a) uqkic   quarrel
    (b) ueneq   question
    (c) tiequ   quiz
    (d) qeeuu   quay
    (e) qyua   quiet
    (f) izuq   quality

(g) toque	queen
(h) tesiounq	quote
(i) yalutiq	queue
(j) realruq	quick

2. SEARCH
Trace these abbreviations in your dictionary or encyclopedia.

Q.C.   Qld   Qantas   q.v.   Q.E.D.

3. WHO AM I?

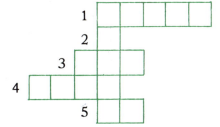

CLUES
1. Opposite of 'loud'
2. Follows 'q'
3. Comes before eleven
4. Synonym for 'friend'
5. Opposite of 'yes'

4. SPELLING
Arrange these words alphabetically, and make sure that you can spell them.

quay	quite	question
quote	quest	quiz
quick	queen	quarrel
quiet	quality	queue

5. TAXI-QUEUE

This game can have two or more players. All you need is dice. The winner is the first to arrive at the taxi rank.

11

5
CH

Some letters and sounds come from different countries. CH is found in the English language, but it is also found in the Greek and French languages.

Remember

CH   when used in English has a hard sound (child, church, chop).

CH   used in the Greek form makes a K sound (chemist, school, Christmas)

CH   used in the French form makes a soft SH sound (chef, chiffon, champagne)

1. DICTIONARY HUNT
   Use your dictionary to find more words for each column.

ENGLISH	GREEK	FRENCH
challenge	chemist	chef
chicken	school	champignon

2. WHICH IS WHICH?
   Copy these words into your workbook. Use blue to mark the hard CH, red to mark the soft CH, and green to mark CH which sounds like K.

chop	child	chef	cheap
scholar	chronic	chat	technical
machine	cheap	cheque	church
Christmas	merchant	chemistry	technology
mechanic	chemical	scholarship	much
chauffeur	choose	such	chocolate
punch	machinist	kitchen	chill
crochet	which	itch	challenge
chance	change	chivalry	French
ache	starch	torch	teacher

3. WHAT AM I?
   CLUES
   1. Which language uses CH as a SH sound?
   2. Another word for clergyman
   3. An institution where learning takes place
   4. Which language uses CH as a K sound?

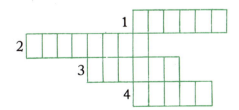

13

4. SNAP
   Make cards using the words you found in DICTIONARY HUNT. Play snap as usual, matching words according to the country of origin.

5. SPELLING
   Arrange these words alphabetically, and make sure that you can spell them.

chemist	chauffeur	mechanic
merchant	technical	cheap
scholar	chocolate	Christmas
ache	crochet	cheque

6
PH

Letters, like people, are influenced by their friends. Some letters behave differently in the company of other letters. When P and H come together they make a completely different sound.

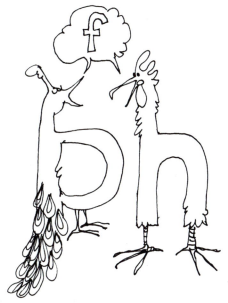

Remember
P + H makes an F sound.   Phillip   elephant   prophet

1. DICTIONARY HUNT
   Use your dictionary to find:
   (a) 10 words that begin with PH.
   (b) 10 words that contain PH.

2. MIX AND MATCH

Match these words with their meanings. You may need the help of your dictionary.

	WORD	MEANING
(a)	phantom	A plant that has clusters of flowers
(b)	pharmacy	Not true; false; imitation
(c)	pheasant	Image or illusion
(d)	philately	A gamebird
(e)	phlox	Stamp collecting
(f)	phoney	Chemist shop

3. DETECTIVE WORK

One word in this paragraph is an exception to the rule. Which word is it?

The sun had set. The night was fresh but still. The moon was in its last phase. Phillip the shepherd looked once again over his flock. All was well, and he would sleep that night. His philosophy was simple: unless there was a full moon, preying animals would not bother him.

4. ELEPHANT JOKES

How many elephant jokes do you know?
Collect as many elephant jokes as you can.

Q. How do you fit four elephants into a mini?

A. Simple! Two in the front, two in the back and the trunks in the boot.

5. SPELLING

Make sure you can spell these words.

pheasant	phantom	phrase
telephone	photograph	megaphone

7

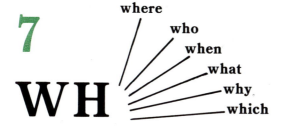

WH — where / who / when / what / why / which

These are location words. They all begin with a 'whirr' sound, except WHO. Notice that WHO has a silent beginning.

1. BLANKS

Copy these sentences and fill in the missing words.

(a) .... time is it?

(b) I will start the barbecue ....they arrive.

(c) I don't know ....colour I prefer.

(d) .... did you do that?

(e) ....said that?

(f) I don't know .... I feel so tired.

(g) I left records on the table. ....are they now?

(h) I don't know ....to wear.

17

(i) ....did that?

(j) I don't know ....pair of jeans to wear.

2. INVISIBLE WORDS

Copy the WH words into your workbook, leaving off the W. What do you get? Now complete the following nonsense sentences.

(a) Who is a ....with the W left off.

(b) When is a ....with the W left off.

(c) What is a ....with the W left off.

(e) Why is a ....with the W left off.

(f) Which is a ....with the W left off.

3. FIND A WORD

How many words beginning with WH can you find? Some words appear twice.

W	E	T	M	K	N	D	W	H	O
B	H	S	F	H	P	M	E	H	K
R	K	Y	E	W	H	Y	S	I	O
D	C	L	V	H	A	W	T	T	F
F	Y	W	P	E	W	H	A	T	S
I	J	H	H	N	S	I	G	W	L
W	H	E	N	A	O	C	R	H	N
E	T	R	E	H	T	H	W	I	J
L	V	E	W	H	E	R	E	C	L
W	A	X	H	T	C	H	W	H	Y

4. USE YOUR IMAGINATION
   (a) What is her name?
   (b) Why do you think she is walking down this street?
   (c) Which house is hers?
   (d) Where do you think she is going?
   (e) When do you think she was born?

8

Y

Y is sometimes a vowel and sometimes a consonant. When Y begins a word it is a consonant. Every other time is it a vowel. Notice how it makes a different sound.

1. AM I A VOWEL? AM I A CONSONANT?
    Draw two columns in your workbook — one for vowels, one for consonants.

you	sky	trying
sunny	pay	many
buy	why	yellow
Friday	hurry	yet
your	wayward	happy
yesterday	flying	money
year	yield	haystack

2. ODD WORD OUT
    Pick out the word which does not follow the rule.

(a) ·	pay	yes	day
(b)	my	yet	you
(c)	year	yellow	why
(d)	reply	Mary	young
(e)	yell	fancy	Tuesday
(f)	yacht	yoga	money
(g)	yearn	wary	try
(h)	fly	yard	yesterday
(i)	yawn	sunny	stay
(j)	youth	worry	rainy

3. MAKE A JINGLE

    Hey, it's pay day.

    Hurry funny Harry.

    Yesterday you yelled.

    Over to you!

4. WORD SEARCH

How many words can you find? You may move in any direction, but only one square at a time.

9

EA/AI/IE/EI

When two vowels go walking, the first one does the talking.

Remember
EA says E
AI says A
IE says I
EI says E

1. DICTIONARY HUNT
   Use your dictionary to help you finish the following chart.

EA	AI	IE	EI
each	pain	pie	deceive

2. PICK THE ODD WORD
   All rules are made to be broken. Find the exceptions to the rule.

   (a) leave   early   preach
   (b) teacher   beach   search
   (c) pieman   lie   believe
   (d) ceiling   deceive   neighbour
   (e) paint   plain   air
   (f) tried   view   cried
   (g) lean   meal   team
   (h) fair   brain   strain
   (i) flies   piece   fried
   (j) said   cream   drain

3. WHAT AM I?
   CLUES
   1. Half a dozen
   2. Abbreviation for a member of parliament
   3. Ours has 26 letters
   4. A number which is an exception to the EI rule
   5. A naming word

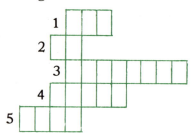

4. WORD BUILDING
   Here is a house with EA/AI/IE/EI words joined at the corners. What can you make? Here are some ideas.
   (a) book
   (b) package
   (c) chair
   (d) table

```
                d
            i       e
          a           a
        s   a   i   l
        e           e
        a           a
        m   a   i   n
```

5. I SPY
   Play this game the usual way, naming vowel sounds.

   • I spy with my little eye something that has
     EA/AI/IE/EI.

10
OA/OE/UE/UI

These are less common vowel combinations, but they still follow the same rule as EA/AI/IE/EI. The first vowel is the more important and makes more noise.

Remember
OA says O
OE says O
UE says U
UI says U

1. DICTIONARY HUNT
   Use your dictionary to help you finish the following chart.

OA	OE	UE	UI
soap	toe	due	juice

2. WHAT'S THE DIFFERENCE?
   Check the meanings of these words. Then use them in sentences of your own.

   (a) cue   (b) tomato   (c) moat
       clue   potato   boat

3. UNSCRAMBLE
   Match the mixed-up letters with their pairs.

   (a) talof   goat
   (b) secunina   doe
   (c) reedove   bruise
   (d) ogat   throat
   (e) edo   nuisance
   (f) resubi   fuel
   (g) eluf   float
   (h) rattho   overdue

4. SUE AND PRUE
    Somewhere in this puzzle Sue and Prue are hidden.
    You'll find Joe at 7(a), 8(b), 9(c).

	1	2	3	4	5	6	7	8	9	10
(a)	S	O	R	W	B	F	J	T	R	N
(b)	U	F	H	A	J	D	S	O	E	I
(c)	D	S	E	I	N	A	T	M	E	X
(d)	G	K	U	Y	S	Y	C	R	B	U
(e)	Q	C	L	E	D	N	H	G	A	Z
(f)	A	T	M	S	P	R	J	K	I	O
(g)	W	L	H	Z	O	U	G	E	Q	W
(h)	N	Y	C	B	D	T	U	D	A	S
(i)	S	U	L	G	A	R	B	F	M	Y
(j)	J	I	E	X	P	E	M	H	P	T

5. TOASTED OR ROASTED?
    Copy this chart into your workbook, adding as many
    things as you can think of to the chart.

TOASTED	ROASTED
crumpets	pumpkin

11

OO

Remember

OO has two sounds

FOOT
(short sound)

TOOL
(long sound)

1. ODD WORD IN

    Pick the odd word in each line.

(a)	book	took	moon
(b)	soon	fool	boom
(c)	pool	shook	soot
(d)	room	brook	nook
(e)	crook	broom	loom
(f)	shook	tool	wood
(g)	cool	too	zoo
(h)	moor	booth	tooth
(i)	smooth	door	choose
(j)	stood	snooze	zoom

2. WORD-BUILDING
   Here is a staircase.
   What can you build?
   Here are some suggestions.
   (a) city skyline
   (b) bridge
   (c) truck
   (d) geometric design

```
                                    C
                                    O
                                    O
                                 BROOK
                                    O
                                    O
                                 LOOM
                                    O
                                    O
                               SHOOK
                                  O
                             M    O
                             TOOK
                               O
                          SPOON
                             O
                             O
                          FOOL
```

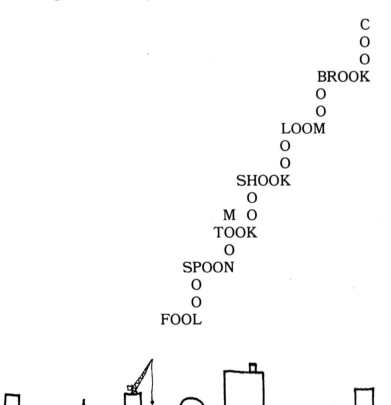

3. WHAT AM I?
    CLUES
    1. The sixth letter of the alphabet
    2. The weather in summer is ....
    3. Opposite of clue 2
    4. The silent letter in 'half'

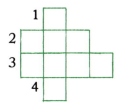

4. SNAP
    Using words from 'Odd word in', make cards with short and long OO sounds. Play Snap in the usual way, matching sounds.

12

The OI Boys

It's very hard to tell the difference between OI and OY. OY is usually last, while OI is usually in the middle.

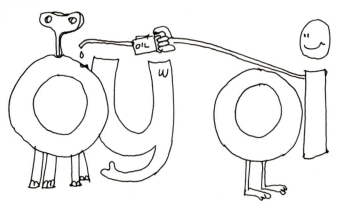

1. DICTIONARY HUNT
   Use your dictionary to help you finish the following chart.

OY	OI
annoy	poison

2. MISSING WORDS
   Fill in the blank spaces with the best word from the box.

point	soy	soil	joint
enjoy	boil	spoil	Roy

(a) Have the vegetables come to the .... ?

(b) I ....going to see a movie.

(c) My friend .... and I are going to Luna Park.

(d) Last week at baseball I hurt my knee ....

(e) Do you like .... sauce on Chinese food?

(f) Please don't .... my secret.

(g) Has anyone seen my ball ....pen?

3.   WHAT'S THE DIFFERENCE?
     Check the meanings of the following words. Then use
     them in sentences of your own.
     (a) employer
     (b) employee
     (c) employment

4.   WHAT AM I?
     CLUES
     1. Opposite of 'empty'
     2. A synonym of 'sea'
     3. A letter that can be either a vowel or a consonant
     4. There are 5 of these in this puzzle
     5. The number of seasons in a year

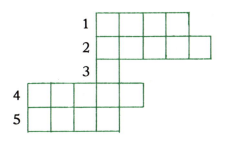

33

5. DISAPPOINTMENT
   (2 or more players)
   This game is like a normal dice game, except that the first player to reach the finish is the loser. The winner is the last player to finish!

You stayed behind after class to help the teacher tidy the room. Return to START.

You helped your young brother with his homework. Return to START.

You wagged school one afternoon. Have another turn.

You did yard duty this week. Miss one turn.

You have been cheeky to the teacher. Advance 3 spaces.

You got your homework all right. Miss one turn.

13

The **ER** Gang

The ER gang wear the same clothes, and do and say the same things. We must get to know them well before we can tell them apart.

1. DICTIONARY HUNT
   Use your dictionary to help you complete the following chart.

ER	IR	UR
fern	girl	surf

2. WHO AM I?
   CLUES
   1. Number of years in a decade
   2. Midday meal
   3. Traffic colour indicating 'stop'
   4. C makes this sound when followed by E/I/Y
   5. Another way to spell 'blew'

3. MISSING WORDS
   Fill in the blank spaces with the best word from the box.

stern	shirts	fur	sunburnt
purse	Saturday	third	turkey

   (a) My family is planning to go on a picnic next ....
   (b) On a winter's day my .... coat keeps the cold out.
   (c) Our team came ....in the school relay.
   (d) I wash and iron my own ....to help my mother.
   (e) Because I have fair skin I must be careful not to get .... at the beach.
   (f) I will give a reward to anyone who finds my ....
   (g) We had a ....for Christmas dinner.
   (h) Our school principal is very ....

4. LUCKY DIP
   Write out sentences using words from 'Missing Words' on strips of cardboard. Cut them into individual words. Each player takes a turn at dipping. The winner is the first one to complete a sentence.

14

OW and OU

Both OW and OU can make the same sound. They also make other sounds.

1. MISSING WORDS

    Fill in the blank spaces with the best word from the box.

town	scouts	prowler	about
mountain	down	trout	frown

    (a) The old lady tripped as she went .... the stairs.
    (b) I'll be ready .... 7 o'clock.
    (c) My father goes fishing and often brings home ....
    (d) This .....has a population of approximately 15,000.
    (e) When we saw the footsteps we suspected the noise
        we heard had been a ....

38

(f) My brother wants me to join his ....climbing club.
(g) Many people .... when they have a problem.
(h) The ....in our suburb are having a bottle drive.

2. FIND THE ODD ONE
    OW can make another sound. Pick out the words with the odd OW.

grow	slow	how
now	brown	know
cow	row	own
slow	owl	low
towel	snow	blow
yellow	growl	fellow

3. FIND THE ODD OU
    OU can make several sounds. Pick out the odd OU.

bough	bound	through
sour	rough	tough
bought	spout	thought
round	snout	cough
nought	now	how
lout	about	trough

4. UNSCRAMBLE
    Match the mixed-up letters with the correct word.

(a) uto	ground
(b) nrdugo	flour
(c) bsoerw	round
(d) tobua	meadow
(e) lowpr	bough
(f) wedamo	out
(g) gohub	prowl
(h) ufrol	owl
(i) donur	browse
(j) wlo	about

5. WHAT DOES THE COW SAY?
   Make a jingle to reply to the farmer.

15
AW and AU

AU and AW are confused because they often sound alike.

1. DICTIONARY HUNT
   Use your dictionary to help you complete the following chart.

AU	AW
sauce	prawn

2. MISSING WORDS
   Fill in the blank spaces with the best word from the box.

audio	automatic	jaw	crawl
Paul	claws	cause	raw

(a) Cigarette smoking can .... cancer.

(b) My father's new car is ....

(c) The prize boxer fell down after he was hit on the ....

(d) Little babies usually ...... before they learn to walk.

(e) My best friend .... is starting his first job tomorrow.

(f) The eagle held a young bird in its ....

(g) Our school has a lot of expensive .... equipment.

(h) Some people are allergic to ....meat.

3. UNSCRAMBLE
    Match the mixed-up letters with the correct word.

(a) ward	naughty
(b) boomautile	awful
(c) gatuth	law
(d) hynagut	automobile
(e) awl	because
(f) warst	taught
(g) saubeec	draw
(h) fawlu	straw

4. WHO AM I?

    CLUES
    1. A synonym for 'mad'
    2. Follows a question
    3. .... of kin
    4. Used for camping
    5. Australian domestic airline

    6. 100 years
    7. Opposite of 'dark'
    8. 12 months
    9. Usually the first word a baby says
    10. Abbreviation for 'Australia'

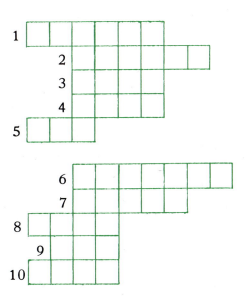

16
CH or TCH

CH and TCH make the same sound and are often confused. There is no easy way to remember when to use CH or TCH. The best way is to become familiar with the spelling of words that contain these sounds.

1. INSIDE WORDS

```
              LID
              |
     DIE         HILL
LIE      CHILLED      DILL
     IDLE         LED
              |
              ILL
```

How many words can you find inside these words?

catch	chalk	hitch	bachelor
thatch	watch	chimney	change

2. MIX AND MATCH
Join the beginnings to their endings.

(a) RI	TCH
(b) PA	CH
(c) SU	CH
(d) MU	TCH
(e) CRU	CH
(f) FE	TCH
(g) LA	CH
(h) EA	TCH

3. WHO AM I?

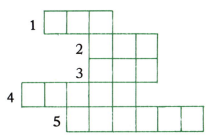

CLUES
1. Opposite of 'old'
2. Another word for 'sick'
3. Another way to spell 'too'
4. Tells the time
5. A place of worship
   (begins and ends the same way)

45

4. I Spy

   Play the game according to the following examples.

   - I spy with my little eye a word ending with CH/TCH.
   - I spy with my little eye a word that begins (or contains) CH.

5. Spelling

   Make sure that you can spell these words.

church	latch	wrench
rich	Scotch	each
chased	pitch	much
bachelor	crutch	sandwich

17
IGHT or ITE

There is no easy way to remember when to use IGHT or ITE. The best way is to use these words as often as possible to become familiar with them.

1. MIX AND MATCH
   Match the beginnings with their endings.

Beginnings	Endings
(a) s	ight
(b) pl	ight
(c) k	ite
(d) qu	ite
(e) m	ight
(f) sp	ight
(g) n	ite
(h) b	ite
(i) wh	ight
(j) f	ite

2. WORD-BUILDING

Here are the letters L, Z, and N. Note that the last letter of one word is the first letter of the next word, and so on. How many letters can you build? Here are some suggestions.

E / F / H / K / T / V / W / X / Y

```
l
i
g
h
t   i   g   h   t


r   i   g   h   t
            h
        g
    i
s   i   t   e


b               t
i   i           i
t       g       g
e           h   h
                t
```

3. WHAT AM I?
   1. Slang word for 'movies'
   2. An old milk bottle size
   3. Coffee or ....?
   4. Makes honey

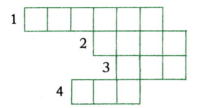

4. SNAP
   Make cards using words from 'Mix and Match' and any extra words you can think of. Play snap in the usual way, matching ITE or IGHT endings.

5. SPELLING
   Make sure you can spell these words.

fight	alight
slight	mighty
bites	rite
rights	quite

18
TION

Arrange for someone to test your spelling of the following words.

combustion	conclusion
nation	ignition
fashion	station
electrician	completion
mission	motion

If you got them all right, miss units 18, 19 and 20 (TION, SION, CIAN)

1. DICTIONARY HUNT
   Use your dictionary to find five words for each column.

ATION	ITION	OTION	ETION	UTION
station	petition	potion	deletion	absolution

2. MISSING WORDS
   Fill the blanks with the correct word.
   (a) My cousin is a .... [notion, relation]
   (b) I have found a .... to the problem.
       [solution, condition]
   (c) When I leave school, my .... is to be a pilot.
       [ambition, contribution]
   (d) I feel comfortable sitting in this ....
       [solution, position]
   (e) I wonder who will win the ....
       [competition, distribution]

(f) The ....of Australia is small when compared to that of other countries. [addition, population]

(g) .... will be held for the school play next week. [auditions, positions]

(h) It is important to use suntan .... when at the beach. [lotion, potion]

3. MIX AND MATCH

Match the beginnings with their endings.

(a) poll		ition
(b) em		ution
(c) ign		ation
(d) dict		otion
(e) compl		ation
(f) st		etion
(g) cond		ution
(h) sol		ition

4. WORDS WITHIN WORDS

How many words can you find using the following words?

(a) composition
(b) addition
(c) population

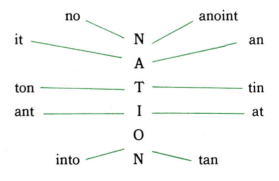

no — N — anoint
it — N — an
A
ton — T — tin
ant — I — at
O
into — N — tan

5. SPELLING
   Make sure that you can spell these words.

elation	completion
position	pollution
detention	intention
addition	subtraction

19
SION

Beware! SION has the same sound as TION.

1. DICTIONARY HUNT
   Use your dictionary to find more words for each column.

ASION	ISION	ESION	OSION	USION
invasion	vision	lesion	corrosion	confusion

2. MIX AND MATCH
   Match the beginnings with their endings.

(a) adh	asion
(b) concl	esion
(c) telev	osion
(d) occ	usion
(e) er	ision
(f) expl	asion
(g) inv	ision
(h) rev	osion

3. WHAT'S THE DIFFERENCE?
   Check the meanings of the following words. Then use
   them in sentences of your own.
   (a) allusion
   (b) illusion
   (c) delusion

4. WHAT AM I?
   CLUES
   1. Opposite of 'last'
   2. Last vowel in the alphabet
   3. Same as 'apologetic'
   4. Another way of spelling 'eye'
   5. A green light gives this signal
   6. Source of heat

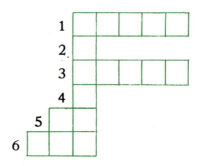

5. WORDS WITHIN WORDS

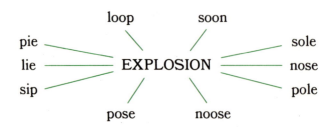

54

How many words can you find in the following words?
(a) television
(b) confusion
(c) occasion

20
CIAN

CIAN sounds like TION and SION. However, there is a magic way to remember when to use CIAN. Just add CIAN to MAGI. What do you get?

Remember
CIAN means a person who practices a particular skill or job.

1. WHAT DO I DO?
   Complete the following. You may need to use your dictionary.
   (a) A MUSICIAN is a person who ....
   (b) An ELECTRICIAN is a person who ....

(c) A MATHEMATICIAN is a person who ....
(d) A POLITICIAN is a person who ....
(e) A TECHNICIAN is a person who ....
(f) A BEAUTICIAN is a person who ....
(g) A STATISTICIAN is a person who ....
(h) A DIETICIAN is a person who ....

2. WHAT'S THE DIFFERENCE?
    Check the meaning of the following words. Then use them in sentences of your own.
    (a) physician
    (b) obstetrician
    (c) paediatrician

3. WHO AM I?
    CLUES
    1. 60 minutes make an ....
    2. Opposite of 'down'
    3. French for 'small'
    4. Very cold water
    5. Female version of 'actor'
    6. Babies drink this.
    7. A boy grows into a ....
    8. Another way to spell 'won'

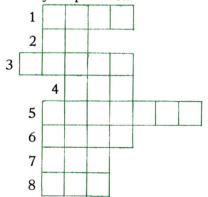

4. REVISION
   Choose a word ending in TION, SION or CIAN.

television	potion	confusion
magician	illusion	explosion

   The .... had left his audience in .... Was it
   just an .... or had the magic .... really worked?
   A few minutes before the white rabbit was sitting
   inside his top hat. All of a sudden there was an ....
   and the hat was empty! It was just like on ...., only
   we had seen it with our own eyes.

5. SPELLING
   Make sure you can spell these words.

technician	musician
physician	mathematician
electrician	beautician
politician	optician

21
ING

- *What do you get when you add ING to JUMP?*
- *What do you get when you add ING to TAKE?*

Why does the E get dropped from the end of TAKE?
(The answer is at the bottom of page 61.)

1. ADDING
   Complete the following chart.

(a)	take	taking	(k)	yell	yelling
(b)	make		(l)	tell	
(c)	hope		(m)	sell	
(d)	rake		(n)	smell	
(e)	like		(o)	call	
(f)	wake		(p)	fall	
(g)	joke		(q)	roll	
(h)	bake		(r)	spell	
(i)	vote		(s)	poll	
(j)	cope		(t)	sniff	

2. ARE YOU TRICKED?
Explain why the following words are exceptions to the rule.

(a) love   (b) have   (c) shove

3. VOWEL SOUNDS
Copy these words into your workbook, marking the vowel sounds as shown:

- lāke   (long sound)
- hĭll   (short sound)

(a) dull	(d) spill	(g) flat	(j) top	(m) bell
(b) spoke	(e) tap	(h) spike	(k) nude	(n) hike
(c) kill	(f) Pete	(i) late	(l) home	(o) mud

4. DO IT NOW
Rewrite the following sentences, using the example as a model.

- I will bake a chocolate cake for your birthday.
- I am baking a chocolate cake for your birthday.

(a) My family will sell their house when we all leave home.
(b) My father will come to see me swim at the school sports.
(c) My brother will buy a car when he gets his driver's licence.
(d) I will take an extra pair of bathing togs in case everyone wants to go for a swim.
(e) I will go home when it gets dark.

5. BINGO
- *Players make 25 individual word cards to fit squares on a bingo board. The words must all come from this unit.*

- *Each player covers the bingo board with word cards at random. The caller names a vowel — indicating whether it has a short or long sound.*
- *Players cross out any square which has the correct sound. The winner is the first player to cover five squares in any one direction.*

When a word contains a long vowel sound, the E is dropped before adding ING.

22

Plurals

Remember

Singular means only one.   I have one hat.
Plural means more than one.   I have three hats.

Three ways to make plurals:

• **In most cases, to make a plural, add S.**

        hat   hats
        dog   dogs

• **When a word ends in S, X, CH, SH, add ES.**

        boss   bosses
        box   boxes
        porch   porches
        dish   dishes

• **When a word ends in Y, change Y to I and add ES.**

        baby   babies
        lady   ladies

1. MORE
   Complete the following chart.

	Singular	Plural			Singular	Plural
(a)	house			(h)	gas	
(b)	church			(i)	candy	
(c)	maid			(j)	dress	
(d)	desk			(k)	tree	
(e)	fish			(l)	bunch	
(f)	miss			(m)	horse	
(g)	grape			(n)	glass	

2. SINGULAR TO PLURAL
   Rewrite the following sentences, changing the words in bold black type to plural. You will also need to alter some other words.
   (a) This **flower** is very attractive.
   (b) My **shoelace** is broken.
   (c) I can see a **fish** swimming under the pier.
   (d) I will need a **match** to light the fire.
   (e) Would you pass me that empty **box**?
   (f) I would like some **candy** for my birthday.

3. PLURAL TO SINGULAR
   (a) Take some **apples** with you.
   (b) What are your favourite **lollies**?
   (c) Some **churches** are very historic.
   (d) My favourite **books** are about animals.
   (e) Bring some **torches** to let us see in the dark.
   (f) I've got some spare **pencils** if you need any.

4. BINGO
   • Players make individual word cards to fit the 25 squares on the bingo board. All the words must come from this unit. Words may be chosen at random, but

each player must have both singular and plural words.

- Players cover their bingo boards with their word cards. The caller names a word from this unit, choosing either its singular or plural form. Players cross out squares with the correct words.
- The winner is the first player to cover five squares in any direction.

23

Double Consonants

- If you add ING to JUMP,
  what do you get? **jumping**
- If you add ING to HOP,
  what do you get? **hopping**

Why do we double the P in 'hopping' and not in 'jumping'?

Remember

One-syllable words which have a short vowel sound and a final single consonant must double the final consonant before adding ING/ED/ER (and the less common endings EST/Y/ISH/EN).

1. ING, ED, ER

   Complete the following chart.

		ing	ed	er
(a)	slip			
(b)	skip			
(c)	weed			
(d)	mob			
(e)	snoop			
(f)	shop			
(g)	pat			
(h)	bump			
(i)	trip			
(j)	call			

2. ADD Y

   Change the word in bold black type to a word ending in Y.

   (a) This bed has **lumps** in it. It is ....

   (b) The weather has a **nip** in it! It is ....

   (c) My brother is **fat**. We call him ....

   (d) This road has many **bumps**. It is ....

   (e) Look at the gorgeous **sun**! I love ....days.

   (f) Our teacher has the **grumps**. He is ....

3. WHO AM I?

   Match the definitions with the right person from the box.

teacher	preacher	jogger	robber

   (a) A person who delivers sermons

   (b) A person who takes things that do not belong to him

   (c) A person who instructs pupils

   (d) A person who runs regularly to improve his health

4. WORDS WITHIN WORDS

   How many words can you find in the following words?

   (a) slipping
   (b) grinning
   (c) shipping
   (d) stopping
   (e) funny

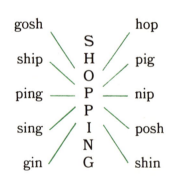

66

24

Punctuation

Q – Why do we have a traffic code?
A – Because it helps us make sense of the road.

Q – Why do we have a writing code (punctuation)?
A – Because it helps us make sense of writing.

full stop

Remember

. A FULL STOP is like a STOP SIGN because it tells us to halt.

, A COMMA is like a CAUTION LIGHT because it tells us to pause.

? A QUESTION MARK is like an S BEND because we don't know what is coming next.

! AN EXCLAMATION MARK is like a DANGER SIGN because we must pay attention.

" TALKING MARKS are like WARNING SIGNS because they let us know something is important.

1. MIX AND MATCH
Match the pairs, then copy them into your workbook.

pedestrian crossing

keep left

T-junction

curve

2. PUNCTUATION
Rewrite these sentences with punctuation marks.
(a) John Peter Sam and Tom all went to a movie
(b) Stand up
(c) Where are you going
(d) Stop talking in class said the teacher
(e) I like all fruit except bananas
(f) Help me
(g) I don't like geography do you
(h) Fares please said the tram conductor

3. PARAGRAPH
When you begin a new sentence you must use a capital letter. Also, begin a new paragraph when a different person speaks.

Susan and her friend Jenny were both very excited about starting school again after the summer holidays they were going to be in form 3 and would no longer be treated as juniors why are you both so excited asked Susan's mother all those gorgeous boys sighed Susan wow replied Jenny.

4. WHAT AM I?
CLUES
1. Americans call it an automobile
2. Opposite of 'in'
3. One third of a school year
4. Question ....
5. First letter of the alphabet

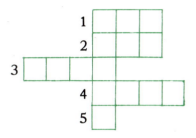

5. DETECTIVE
How many traffic signs can you spot?

25

Contractions

When we speak, we often slide two words together. This is called a CONTRACTION. We show this in writing by using an apostrophe. The apostrophe shows us where one or more letters have been left out.

- IT IS   IT'S   (I has been left out)
- IS NOT   ISN'T   (O has been left out)

1. SHORTENING
   Make contractions of the following:

   (a) are not   (g) does not
   (b) do not   (h) were not
   (c) have not   (i) you are
   (d) did not   (j) could not
   (e) was not   (k) would not
   (f) I am   (l) should not

2. EXPANDING
Write out the full form of these contractions.

(a) you've   (h) we've
(b) I've   (i) she's
(c) I'll   (j) you'll
(d) we're   (k) who's
(e) here's   (l) can't
(f) I'd   (m) let's
(g) what's   (n) won't

3. TRUE OR FALSE?
Decide which is true and which is false. Write both sentences in your workbooks with T or F in brackets.

(a) I didn't do my homework last night.
    I did do my homework last night.   ( )
    I did not do my homework last night.   ( )

(b) The band won't be playing at the dance.
    The band will be playing at the dance.   ( )
    The band will not be playing at the dance.   ( )

(c) He's very good looking.
    He is very good looking.   ( )
    He is not very good looking.   ( )

(d) My mother said I can't go with you to the beach.
    My mother said I cannot go with you to the beach.   ( )
    My mother said I can go with you to the beach.   ( )

(e) You weren't at the school social on Friday.
    You were at the school social on Friday.   ( )
    You were not at the school social on Friday.   ( )

(f) I'm feeling great because the holidays are here.
I am not feeling great because the holidays are here. ( )
I am feeling great because the holidays are here. ( )

(g) I'll be there about 7.30 tonight.
I will be there about 7.30 tonight. ( )
I will not be there about 7.30 tonight. ( )

(h) I wasn't sure you played sport.
I was not sure you played sport. ( )
I was sure you played sport. ( )

(i) I'm sorry I couldn't make it to your party.
I am sorry I could make it to your party. ( )
I am sorry I could not make it to your party. ( )

(j) We're going to arrive on time.
We are not going to arrive on time. ( )
We are going to arrive on time. ( )

4. PARAGRAPH
Change as many words as you can to make contractions. Remember to start a new paragraph when a different person speaks.

'It is such a beautiful day, let us go to the beach,' suggested Tony to his family. 'Not today, I am sorry. We have to visit Grandpa,' replied Tony's mother. 'What is wrong with Grandpa?' asked Tony's sister. 'He is very ill at present and likes us to visit him.'

5. ARE YOU TRICKED?
Make contractions of the following pairs.

(a) I had   (c) He/she is
(b) I would   (d) He/she has

26

Apostrophe S

There are two simple rules for using an apostrophe
S ('S).
The main thing to remember is that an apostrophe
S shows ownership or possession.

RULE 1

• **Singular possession — add 'S.**

    This is Tony's book.

However, if the word already ends in S, you can add
only an apostrophe.

    This is Ross's book.

    This is Ross' book.

RULE 2

• **Plural possession — add an apostrophe.**

    These are the boys' books.

•   However, if the plural form of the word does not end
in S, you simply add 'S.

    These are the children's books.

1. INSERT
   Add an apostrophe (where necessary).
   (a) I like my grandmothers fruit cake.
   (b) Louis is moving to a new school.
   (c) Where is the mens cloakroom?
   (d) My grandfather is eighty next birthday.
   (e) Do you like Ross new jeans?
   (f) Would the ladies please be seated?
   (g) My sister-in-laws house is being painted.
   (h) Chris has a new tennis racquet.
   (i) The childrens holidays begin shortly.
   (j) Mrs Joss goes shopping every Friday.

2. PARAGRAPH
   Copy this paragraph into your workbook, adding any apostrophes you think necessary.

   Detective Jones was following the scent of the citys most wanted criminal. He was last seen outside Louis Cafe, near the waterfront, wearing a sailors outfit. What was he up to? There seemed little doubt that he intended to leave the country. Detective Jones intuition told him to lie low and wait for the criminals next move. Detective Jones would be waiting.

3. LUCKY DIP
   Write out five sentences from 'Insert' on long strips of cardboard. Cut the strips into individual words. Each player dips for a card until someone can make one of the sentences.

4. WHAT AM I?

   CLUES
   1. The only letter in the alphabet that does not have a letter before it.

2. Opposite of 'shut'
3. An exclamation
4. Often found with a cup
5. Abbreviation of 'street'
6. Abbreviation of 'road'
7. Where animals are kept in captivity for the public to see
8. A stone fruit
9. Joins P to make an F sound
10. The most common vowel.

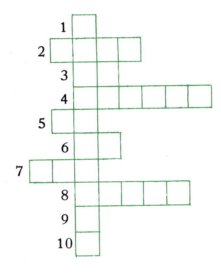

27

Its/It's/Isn't

You will notice in the unit on apostrophe S that we did not use IT'S. This is because IT'S is an exception to the rule. It does not show possession.

"I, must?.use!,proper: punctuation!,?.

it's an elephant!

Remember

The only time we can use IT'S is when it stands for IT IS. If it makes sense, then use it. If not, it must be wrong. Look at the following examples:

• It's school holidays in a few weeks.
  (It is school holidays in a few weeks).

• The navy is proud of it's new destroyer.
  (The navy is proud of it is new destroyer.)

1. IN OR OUT?
   Add an apostrophe (if necessary).
   (a) The weather forecast says its going to be fine.
   (b) Its my birthday next month.
   (c) Has the dog eaten its dinner?
   (d) I think its your mistake.
   (e) The little baby has its first tooth.
   (f) Its your friend on the telephone.
   (g) My cat lost one of its paws in an accident.
   (h) Its Friday tomorrow.
   (i) Its time to leave.
   (j) I think its raining outside.

Remember

ISN'T is a contraction of IS NOT. We have become so used to using ISN'T that if we say IS NOT, it sometimes sounds old-fashioned and odd. Look at the following examples:
- Isn't it a beautiful day?
  (Is not it a beautiful day?)

- Today is Monday, isn't it?
  (Today is Monday, is not it?)

2. EXPAND
   Copy these sentences into your workbook, using two words instead of the contraction.
   (a) The weather isn't hot enough for swimming.
   (b) Isn't Tom coming with us?
   (c) 'It isn't home time yet,' announced the teacher.
   (d) My pencil sharpener isn't working.
   (e) It is Sunday tomorrow, isn't it?
   (f) The new TV isn't being delivered until next week.
   (g) My best friend isn't at school today.
   (h) 'It isn't fair,' shouted Mark.

3. MISSING WORDS
   Fill in the blanks with either ITS/IT'S/ISN'T.
   (a) I think .... going to rain.
   (b) The cat is busily licking ....paws.
   (c) What a magnificent view, ... it?
   (d) My best friend .... very well today.
   (e) The score is very close. .... going to be a
       cliff-hanger.
   (f) .... eleven o'clock now, only one hour until
       midnight.
   (g) The eagle spread .... wings as it soared above.
   (h) This task .... going to be easy.

28

Revision of Units 24, 25, 26, 27

Punctuate these passages:

1. when a passenger complained to a guard about the railways service the guard said if you dont like it why dont you get out and walk i would the passenger replied but i am not expected home until the train arrives

2. a woman found that her wristwatch would not work so she wrote to the manufacturer when she got no answer she sent the company a telegram reading i have one of your watches what time is it that did it they sent her a new watch

3. what impressed you most about the opposing team a reporter asked the losing football coach the coach shook his head in awe the fact that when they ran out on to the field it tilted in their direction he replied

4. a detective asked the bank teller who had been robbed for the third time by the same man if he had noticed anything special about the robber yes he was better dressed each time he replied

5. our greengrocers shop had a display of exotic plants with a notice reading it was dangerous for children to touch these plants when i asked why he replied because i will thump them

6. after several hours of taking his lawnmower apart cleaning it and putting it back together my father found he had one piece left over the lawnmower started first time the extra part seemed to have no function until he tried to turn the mower off

29

Homophones

Homophones are words that sound alike, but are spelt differently and have a different meaning.

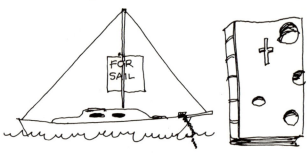

- I think my **eye** has something in it.
- Number **one** has **won** the raffle.

1. SOUNDS SIMILAR
   Find a word with the same sound but different spelling.

   (a) for
   (b) blew
   (c) son
   (d) here
   (e) weak
   (f) hour
   (g) buy
   (h) maid
   (i) mail
   (j) pain
   (k) bear
   (l) knew
   (m) there
   (n) rein

   (o) break
   (p) tail
   (q) holy
   (r) prophet
   (s) soul
   (t) throne
   (u) sum
   (v) sale
   (w) meet
   (x) poor
   (y) fete
   (z) fare
   (aa) hair
   (bb) sow

2. MISSING WORDS
   Fill in the blanks with the correct word.
   (a) My favourite colour is .... [blew, blue]
   (b) Can you .... me clearly? [here, hear]
   (c) I would like to ....a new outfit for the
       occasion. [by, buy]
   (d) The tablets will relieve your .... [pane, pain]
   (e) This looks like your .... [sighs, size]
   (f) Throw your apple ....in the rubbish bin.
       [core, corps]
   (g) In some remote areas the ....is delivered
       only once a week. [male, mail]
   (h) I have .... my exams with .... credits.
       [passed, past /two, too]

3. WHAT'S THE DIFFERENCE?
   Check the meanings of the following homophones.
   Then use them in sentences of your own.
   (a) nun/none   (c) sauce/source
   (b) rapt/wrapped   (d) berth/birth

4. MATCH THE PAIRS
   Pair off each word with the correct set of jumbled
   letters.

BEGINNING	JUMBLED ENDING
(a) sum	aror
(b) there	ums
(c) new	roup
(d) week	irha
(e) pour	reteh
(f) roar	kewe
(g) weather	tise
(h) hair	enw
(i) meat	heetraw
(j) site	eatm

30

Alphabetizing

Can you use a dictionary? Can you use a telephone book? Can you use an index file?

1. SINGLE LETTERS
   Arrange the following letters in alphabetical order.
   You may need to use the list along the edge of the page
   to begin with.

   (a) S E A T M O
   (b) N P B C D E F
   (c) J N K I H D C E
   (d) U C W S P M F G J
   (e) I Q T K R H L O U

2. LETTER COMBINATIONS
   Put the following letter combinations in alphabetical
   order. Note that BA will come before BB, etc.

   (a) BB DD DB BD
   (b) AB BA AA BB DA
   (c) AD DA AA DD DB BA
   (d) MN MM NN NM MA NA AM
   (e) PD BP BB PP PA AP AB BA

3. WORDS
   Put the following words into alphabetical order.
   (a) anger   answer   angle
   (b) dealt   daunt   death   dally
   (c) mouth   moth   month   mould   more
   (d) smell   snack   smack   smoulder   smear
   (e) yet   yes   yell   yellow   yield

4. SHOPPING LIST
   Rewrite this shopping list in alphabetical order.

tea	bread	detergent	carrots
coffee	soap	hairspray	juice
butter	toothpaste	soup	bananas
eggs	milk	chops	salt
rice	flour	honey	apples

5. ANYONE FOR CRICKET?
   Put this cricket team in alphabetical order.

(Back) L. Wit, B. Slog, G. Iggle, F. Donk, X. Limple, B. Bing (12)
(Front) B. Blugg, P. Pobble, G.D.A.B. Sprigg (Capt.), S. Mogwort,
   G. Gump, H. McWhirr

31

Affixes

An affix is an addition to a word. If we add to the beginning of a word we call it a prefix. If we add to the end of a word we call it a suffix. Knowing what the affix means will help you understand the meaning of the word.

1. PREFIX
   Here is a common list of prefixes. Copy these into your workbook. Add two more words to the word column for each prefix.

	PREFIX	MEANING	WORDS
(a)	ab	away from	absent
(b)	anti	against	antidote
(c)	bi	two	biennial
(d)	circum	around	circumference
(e)	contra	against	contraband
(f)	dis	apart	dispute
(g)	ex	out/of	exit
(h)	inter	between	interview
(i)	intro	within	introduce
(j)	mal	bad	malady
(k)	mis	wrong	mistake
(l)	pre	before	prevent
(m)	pro	for/forward	proceed
(n)	re	back/again	return
(o)	sub	under	submerge
(p)	trans	across	transfer
(q)	un	not	untrue

2. SUFFIX

Here is a list of suffixes. Copy these into your work-book. Form a word containing each suffix.

	SUFFIX	WORD		SUFFIX	WORD
(a)	hood		(h)	able	
(b)	ship		(i)	ible	
(c)	ness		(j)	ful	
(d)	ist		(k)	less	
(e)	dom		(l)	ous	
(f)	ment		(m)	ward	
(g)	ant		(n)	ish	

3. MAKE-A-WORD

Using the list above, add a suffix to these words to form a new word. Some words can take more than one suffix, e.g. helpful, helpless.

(a) child   (d) for   (g) dark   (j) help   (m) enjoy
(b) hard   (e) fool   (h) king   (k) care   (n) comfort
(c) false   (f) home   (i) delight (l) kin   (o) self

4. DETECTIVE WORK

Copy these words into your workbook. Underline the part of the word that is a prefix or a suffix.

(a) freedom   (b) toward   (c) transmit
(d) proceed   (e) movement   (f) contradict
(g) terrible   (h) subject   (i) helpless
(j) botanist   (k) unfair   (l) expel
(m) famous   (n) hopeful   (o) retreat
(p) prepare   (q) friendship   (r) marvellous
(s) discover   (t) cyclist

5. WHAT AM I?

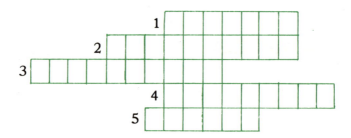

CLUES
1. A sponge does this to water.
2. Opposite of 'fortune'
3. A person who has many achievements is ....
4. You attend one of these before a new job
5. Opposite of 'import'

6. WORD SQUARE

Pick out all the words you can find and write them down in your workbook. Underline each affix.

S	M	A	E	X	P	O	R	T	P
W	O	I	S	C	O	U	E	R	L
E	I	F	P	G	S	D	W	K	U
X	S	S	U	B	T	R	A	C	T
T	R	A	N	S	P	O	R	T	O
R	U	J	O	N	H	B	D	I	W
A	P	R	O	L	O	N	G	X	A
A	T	O	P	A	N	C	S	O	R
M	L	G	O	M	E	W	A	R	D

32

Greek and Latin Derivations

The English language has many sources. Many of our words have been taken from Greek and Latin.

1. GREEK AND LATIN ROOTS

   Here is a list of some common Greek and Latin roots. You will find they are very useful. Copy them into your workbook.

GREEK	MEANING	LATIN	MEANING
grapho	I write	magnus	great
chronos	time	annus	year
tele	far	fluo	flow
auto	self	aqua	water
micros	small	scribo	I write
phone	sound	video	I see
bios	life	moveo	I move
pathos	feeling/suffering	mitto	I send
astro	star	fractus	break
metron	measure	credo	I believe
thermo	heat	audio	I hear
polis	city	specto	I look at
logos	study	bene	good

There are many more Greek and Latin roots which you may wish to add to these lists. Ask your teacher to help you find them.

2. SPOT THE DERIVATION
Underline the section(s) of the word that has a Greek root. Work out the meaning of the word.

Astrology: astro (star) logos (study) The study of the stars.

(a) telegram	(b) chronological	(c) astronaut
(d) microphone	(e) autograph	(f) paragraph
(g) biology	(h) microscope	(i) sympathy
(j) telescope	(k) thermometer	(l) telephone
(m) police	(n) pathology	(o) meter

3. SPOT THE DERIVATION
Underline the part of the word that has a Latin root. Work out the meaning of the word.

(a) audience	(b) fracture	(c) vision
(d) fluid	(e) scribble	(f) credit
(g) anniversary	(h) spectator	(i) movie
(j) aquarium	(k) permit	(l) influence
(m) benefit	(n) fluoride	

4. WORD MAKING
How many words can you make? Each word must have a prefix, root and suffix.

	PREFIX	ROOT	SUFFIX
(a)	ad	capt	(t) ion
(b)	in	vent	or
(c)	inter	sens	(it) ive
(d)	con	posit	ual
(e)	contra	dict	
(f)	de		
(g)	e		

5. BINGO

The rules can be adapted to suit the size of your group.

The caller calls a number. The first student to respond with a word which includes the derivation wins the point. The game is completed when a student has the required number of squares.

1 grapho	2 thermo	3 credo	4 bios	5 micros
6 specto	7 chronos	8 auto	9 mitto	10 tele
11 phone	12 fluo	13 annus	14 scribo	15 polis
16 aqua	17 pathos	18 audio	19 fractus	20 visus
21 metron	22 moveo	23 magnus	24 astro	25 bene

33

Words from other places

English is spoken in many different parts of the world. It is influenced by many other languages.

1. WHERE DO I COME FROM? WHAT DO I MEAN?
   - (a) au revoir
   - (b) bon voyage
   - (c) chef
   - (d) detour
   - (e) nom de plume
   - (f) protégé
   - (g) entrepreneur
   - (h) rendezvous
   - (i) clique
   - (j) valet
   - (k) debut
   - (l) tête-à-tête

2. WHERE DO I COME FROM? WHAT DO I MEAN?
   - (a) prima donna
   - (b) macaroni
   - (c) sonnet
   - (d) pizza
   - (e) capuccino
   - (f) stanza
   - (g) cassata
   - (h) espresso
   - (i) pianoforte
   - (j) ravioli
   - (k) concerto
   - (l) spaghetti

3. MIX AND MATCH
   Pair off the words used in the United States with their equivalent in standard English.

tap	candy	cookies	flat
elevator	apartment	holidays	faucet
rubbish	ketchup	trash	lollies
sauce	biscuits	lift	vacation

4. WHO AM I?
   Give both the common English word and American equivalent.

		AMERICAN	ENGLISH
(a)	I am an invention of the 20th century used for transport		
(b)	I am a season.		
(c)	I am a fuel and can be used for heating.		
(d)	People walk on me.		
(e)	I am used by students to correct mistakes.		

5. TICK THE RIGHT COLUMN

		Person	Place	Animal	Thing
(a)	ocker				
(b)	wowser				
(c)	swagman				
(d)	digger				
(e)	boomerang				
(f)	billabong				
(g)	damper				
(h)	corroboree				

34

Syllables

Breaking words into syllables means breaking words into their vowel sounds. This makes a long word, which looks difficult, easy to pronounce.

silly bull

What To Do

- A, E, I, O, U, and sometimes Y are all vowels. Count the number of vowel sounds in a word.

    YES/TER/DAY has three vowel sounds (syllables).

- Sometimes a word has two vowels but only one vowel sound.

    RAIN has only one vowel sound (syllable).

1. How Many Vowels?

    Copy the words into your workbook, and put the number of vowels after the word in brackets.

    (a) student   (2)

    (b) school

    (c) subject

    (d) period

    (e) teacher

    (f) friend

    (g) English

    (h) history

    (i) dictionary

    (j) holiday

    (k) certificate

    (l) careful

    (m) geography

    (n) science

    (o) Wednesday

    (p) unhappy

2. HOW MANY VOWEL SOUNDS (SYLLABLES)?
   (a) Tuesday (2)   (f) situation   (k) vowel
   (b) easy   (g) once   (l) sound
   (c) nonsense   (h) lettuce   (m) punctuation
   (d) welfare   (i) happily   (n) break
   (e) politics   (j) sentence   (o) many

3. MIX AND MATCH
   Match these syllables with their partners to make words.

	SYLLABLE	PARTNER
(a)	o	swer
(b)	for	zy
(c)	help	tain
(d)	noi	ver
(e)	per	pid
(f)	flow	mit
(g)	cur	er
(h)	an	sy
(i)	la	ful
(j)	stu	get

4. SYLLABLE COUNT
   This is a simple game to play. Make up cards containing words used in this unit. Deal 10 cards to each player. Each player must count the total number of syllables on the cards in their hand. The player with the most wins. You can play a single game or best of 5 games.

35

Compound Words

Compound words are made up of two words joined together.

1. BREAK UP
    Copy these words into your workbook and show where the two words are joined.

    ● mail/man   work/book.

(a) fingernail	(b) outdoor	(c) saucepan
(d) whereabouts	(e) potplant	(f) underwear
(g) sunflower	(h) underneath	(i) booklist
(j) fisherman	(k) barmaid	(l) iceberg
(m) seaman	(n) dressmaking	(o) sunset
(p) newspaper	(q) surfboard	(r) lipstick
(s) railway	(t) teapot	(u) sunshine

2. MIX AND MATCH
    Some compound words are joined together by a hyphen, e.g., good-bye. Match these words with their partners.

spider		apple		office		pillar
	work		on		milk	
stool		box		home		post
	dish		load		washer	
cream		key		shake		see
	ice		web		suit	
wet		note		foot		print
	hole		pie		set	

3. DETECTIVE WORK
   How many compound words can you find?

c	a	n	n	o	t	z	m	i	f
a	r	a	i	l	w	a	y	h	o
r	l	o	k	h	c	m	t	b	o
p	b	q	s	t	k	a	g	c	t
o	t	e	a	s	p	o	o	n	b
r	n	d	u	t	w	e	s	v	a
t	j	r	o	y	c	o	e	j	l
n	s	o	m	h	d	j	r	t	l
j	f	g	e	y	e	l	i	d	q
h	e	a	d	a	c	h	e	a	i

4. UNSCRAMBLE
   *Join up a word from column 1 with a word from column
   2. Give the meaning of the new word.*

	1	2
(a)	cubby	saw
(b)	see	links
(c)	toad	hole
(d)	stage	stool
(e)	cuff	coach

5. ONCE UPON A TIME
   *Here are three compound words that have changed
   their form or meaning over a period. Explain what they
   mean and why we call them compound words.*
   (a) cupboard   (b) shepherd   (c) wardrobe